SAYKI

SAYKI

SAYKI

G et ready to upgrade your dynamic midtown style with timeless pieces from the Sayki 2017 Fall/Winter collection. This season, the collection focuses on key pieces essential for the office but also work for evening commitments. Suits bring back the vest while fur details and denim-inspired shirts are among the must-haves that will help build an individual style. The entire wardrobe is inspired by the balance between opposites. How? Imagine mixing textures, colors and patterns in a single three-piece suit. It works. The customized look you create is yours alone. Sayki dress suits and tuxedos continue to guarantee upscale elegance. The houndstooth pattern graces this season's new pieces and the jackets feature velvet or satin covered lapels. Charcoal, burgundy and navy are the preferred color alternatives to black. If you want black, we have that too. With a collection so wide ranging with many options to update all your looks, Sayki promises not to disappoint in comfort and ease.

We also have a surprise for you in this issue. When you travel to New York next time keep us in mind. Our travel story will get you inspired to tour the city and experience the culinary excellence like the locals do. Istanbul is a part of this inspirational guide as well. The insider's Istanbul will delight tourists and locals alike. Enjoy all your travels this season. We wish you a stylish one.

OWNER
(ON BEHALF OF MIB MAGAZACILIK TIC. A.S.)
HATEM SAYKI
İKİTELLİ ORGANİZE SANAYİ BÖLGESİ, TURGUT ÖZAL
CAD. NO:33 34306, BAŞAKŞEHİR, İSTANBUL

PUBLISHER
DOĞUŞ YAYIN GRUBU
DOĞUŞ CENTER, AHİ EVRAN POLARİS CAD. NO:4
34398 MASLAK/İSTANBUL

PUBLISHING DIRECTOR, SPECIAL PROJECTS
ÖZGE SARIKADILAR
EDITORIAL DIRECTOR
GÜLDENİZ AYRAL
CREATIVE DIRECTOR
HANDE MUMCUOĞLU
SPECIAL PROJECTS MANAGER
İLKE BEYAZ
MANAGING EDITOR
SEDEN MESTAN

CONTRIBUTORS ALİ AKYÜZ, ANIL ALPAY,
BARIŞ ÇAKMAKÇI, DİNÇER DİNÇ, ESEN GÜRAY,
AHMET EMİN HONDOR, SİNAN KARABACAK,
YEŞİM SUÜLKER, DERMAN TAŞKIRAN, PINAR TAVŞAN,
AHU TERZİ, ÇİĞDEM TOPARLAK, HANDE TOPÇU,
MELDA YÜZBAŞIOĞLU

PRINTED AT PROMAT BASIM YAYIN SAN. VE TİC. A.Ş.
PUBLISHED IN TURKEY, SEMI-ANNUALLY

❊ WATCH

Five actors that make the movie

Clive Owen
Croupier (1998)

Jude Law
Alfie (2004)

Michael Fassbender
X-Men (2014)

Steve McQueen
The Thomas Crown Affair (1968)

Tony Servillo
The Great Beauty (2013)

MEN WHO INSPIRE IMPECCABLE STYLE

When the topic is men's style, it might be a good idea to start following a musician, to watch a stylish move or start tracking the style of famous influencers.

8|

❊ FOLLOW

Five influencers who lead on Instagram

The blogger for the 40+ set is David Evans (@greyfoxblog)

Fashion writer and musician Brian Sacawa (@hespokestyle)hespokestyle)

The guide for adding sophisticated details to your style is blogger Matthew Zorpas (@matthewzorpas)

The creative director who likes to break rules (@nickwooster)

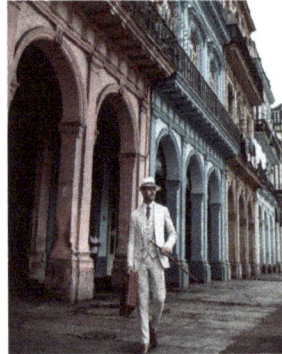

New York Style blogger Adam Gallagher (@iamgalla)

LISTEN
Timeless styles, timeless melodies.

Sam Smith

Robbie Williams

● BY BARIS CAKMAKCI

WINTER SPORTS:

ADRENALINE IN ANATOLIA

SNOW RAFTING – ERZINCAN

Since it's still not widely adopted in Turkey as a winter sport just yet, snow rafting today is truly an adventure opportunity. As you can guess from its name, snow rafting is when you use traditional rafting boats on snow. One of the top ski destinations in Turkey is Ergan Mountain Ski Center, which also boasts the longest piste in Turkey. The elevation is 2970 meters and the center is only 12 km from the Erzincan city center. While the resort only provides daytime accommodations, there are shuttle services between city hotels and the resort. Located on the foothills of the Munzur mountain range, the best snow conditions at Ergan are during winter months, specifically November through March. (ergankayak.com)

HELI-SKI – RIZE

Heli-skiing is off-trail, downhill skiing on remote snow-capped slopes that are accessed by a helicopter. Usually only advanced skiers dare to explore heli-skiing, which can also get expensive very quickly due to the special gear required to navigate through unchartered terrain. A handful of places around the world can actually accommodate heli-skiers and one of these spots is in Ayder Yaylasi in Rize, Turkey. With a peak at
2800 meters, Ayder is actually one of the preferred spots for expert skiers.
(hasimogluotel.com)

SNOWBOARD – SARIKAMIS

The Sarikamis Ski Center features tracks best suited for this popular spot – the locals call it "crystal snow." Some describe it as gliding, or even flying, down the slope as the characteristics of the unique snow help move the snowboard along. The two different tracks accommodate two different expertise levels with their individual gradient. High season is from November through April in Sarikamis, where the surrounding area is covered with a beautiful pine forest. During the season, it snows an average of 57 days and conditions are prime for 141 days. Snow depth is usually around 1.5 meters. (camkarotel.com)

SNOWKITE – ERCIYES

Also known as kiteboarding, this sport combines traditional snowboarding with kitesurfing. It's considered the next step in extreme adventure if you're already an advanced snowboarder. Erciyes Ski Center, which is located 25 km to the Kayseri city center, is considered one of the top destinations for snowkiting in the world. The slopes range between 10-20% at this high altitude resort (3916 meters.) It's actually perfect for both snowboarding and snowkiting with excellent snow conditions during the season lasting from December through April. (kayserierciyes.com.tr)

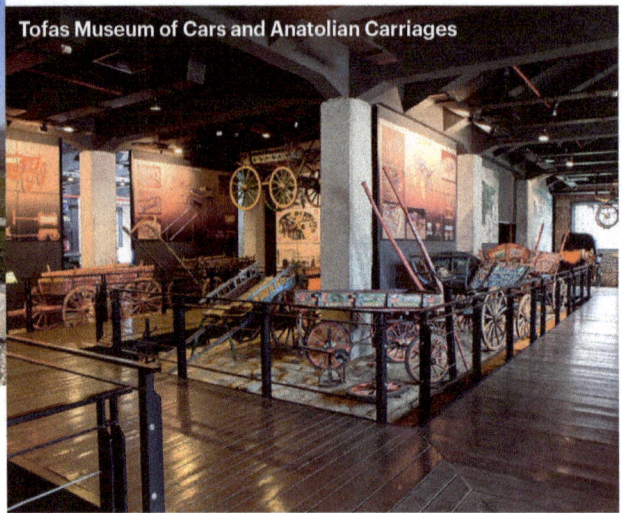
Tofas Museum of Cars and Anatolian Carriages

Baksı Museum

THE ESSENTIAL MUSEUM GUIDE – TURKEY

BAKSI MUSEUM

Located near the Black Sea, 45 km from Bayburt, in the village of Bayraktar, this unique museum brings together a contemporary art collection and traditional handicrafts side by side under one roof. Covering 30 hectares with its exhibition halls, workshop galleries, a conference hall, library and guest houses, the Baksi Museum is the product of Husamettin Kocan, an artist and educator who was born in Bayburt. The museum took home the prestigious Council of Europe Museum Prize in 2014. (baksi.org)

THE COMPLEX OF SULTAN BAYEZID II HEALTH MUSEUM

Another Council of Europe Musuem Prize winner, the complex of Sultan Bayezid II Health Museum is located in Edirne and is made up of several buildings. Originally built in 15th century, the complex contained a Dar al-Shifa (hospital), that was eventually incorporated into Trakya University and converted into a health museum dedicated to the history of medicine and various treatment methods. The museum is the second most visited historical site in Edirne after the Selimiye Mosque. (saglikmuzesi. trakya.edu.tr)

ERIMTAN ARCHEOLOGY AND ARTS MUSEUM

Housing the personal collection of Yuksel Erimtan, the Erimtan Archeology and Arts Museum boasts a diverse collection of artifacts unearthed in Anatolia. Standing near the entrance to the historic Ankara Castle, the museum is inside a newly renovated building whose scale and façade adheres contextually to its historic surrounding. A multi-purpose exhibition hall offers space for temporary exhibitions, scientific, cultural and artistic activities as well as musical concerts. The museum aims to serve the community with its education programs designed for all ages, but especially children. Opening its doors in early 2015, its library provides a rich academic environment for researchers and inquisitive minds alike. Make sure to also check out to the gift shop and café for culinary delights and unique surprises. (erimtanmuseum.org)

CORUM ARCHEOLOGICAL MUSEUM

An archeological museum located in Corum, it was formally established in 1968 with artifacts found in Alacahoyuk, Bogazkoy, Ortakoy, Eskiyapar, Pazarli, Kussaray and Alisar Hoyuk. The collection, amounting to more than 12,000 pieces, is divided into four principal areas, showcasing coins, ceramics, figurines, rugs, clothing, jewelry and other objects from the Hellenistic, Roman, Byzantine, Hittite, Phrygian, Seljuk and Ottoman periods. (muze.gov.tr)

TOFAS MUSEUM OF CARS AND ANATOLIAN CARRIAGES

The Tofaş Museum of Cars and Anatolian Carriages in Bursa is the first and only local automotive museum of Turkey. Located in Umurbey, former silk factory expanding over a 17,000 square meter area was restored by Tofaş and transformed for this purpose. The museum started receiving visitors in 2002. When you tour the building, the entire experience is similar to time travel, with the origins of local automotive production traced back to a single wheel. Today, besides the restored car made in Bursa 2600 years ago, all sorts of motorized vehicles are displayed at the museum, which also serves as physical thank you to the many craftsmen who laid the foundation of this vibrant industry in Bursa. (tofasanadoluarabalarimuzesi.com)

TURKISH AND ISLAMIC ARTS MUSEUM

Located in the famous Sultanahmet Square in Istanbul, the Turkish and Islamic Arts Museum is the first of its kind where the two cultures meet in a single collection. Originally housed within the Suleymaniye Medrese, the collection arrived in its current home in 1983. Constructed in 1524, the building was formerly the palace of Pargali Ibrahim Pasha, who was the second grand vizier to Suleiman the Magnificent. The collection includes notable examples of Islamic calligraphy, tiles, glasswork, ceramics, rugs as well as ethnographic displays on various cultures that existed in Anatolia. (tiem.gov.tr)

Çorum Archeological Museum

10

THE SEASON OF THREE-PIECE SUITS

What every stylish gentleman needs to know about this wardrobe staple

One of the most important trends in the 2017-18 Fall/Winter season is the customized look of a three-piece suit achieved by combining a jacket, a vest and a pair of trousers with different textures, colors and patterns. A classic interpretation of the smart casual style, this personalized look works when put together even if the pieces are not part of the same suit. You can further customize your look to match your individual style by accessorizing your suit with pocket squares, pins and signature ties. If you need to wear a suit to work but want to customize your look by adding your personal style touch, make sure to explore the new colors of the season. Navy and burgundy, traditional gray and charcoal, navy and camel as well as the gray and burgundy combinations are some of the new ways to mix and match with color as your style guide. Woven wool fabrics in honeycomb or multi-color patterns make up the trendiest suits this season. Textured fabrics and monochrome plaid are some of the additional trends that detail the key pieces.

GUIDE TO **FRAGRANCE STYLE**

Fragrance never smells the same on every person. When you spray it on a tester in the store, be sure to note that it may not smell the same on you. In fact, the same perfume may have a different effect on your skin depending on the season. So having a fragrance wardrobe and changing it up each season is not a bad idea. Citrus tones cool during the summer; vanilla and spice goes better in winter months. The top notes in Hatemoglu 1924 include ginger, bergamot, lavender, lemon and peach and the middle notes feature floral additions such as jasmine and freesia. But the deep base notes of leather, musk, sandalwood and amber found in this fragrance make it so suitable for cold weather.

HATEMOGLU

13

SAYKI

SAYKI

The first look at the season

Street looks and the athleisure trend increase their influence on both the classic and casual fashion this season. Asymmetrical prints, large-scale patterns, various fabrics and textures used in trims and other details, color blocks and oversized fits are some of the key influences of the street on what we're seeing in stores today.

EDITOR AHMET EMIN HONDOR

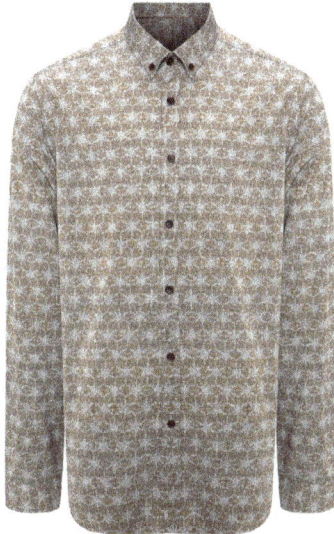

Shirt $ 89,90

Coat
$ 495,00

Scarves (each)
$ 89,90

ARTISTIC PATTERNS

Patterns this season channel an artist's canvas, as if calculated yet random brushstrokes form the elevated designs. Largely used in accessories, these prints play well in both modern and more vintage styles. Try to pair a key print piece with a more natural wardrobe in order to have it stand out.

Pocket Square
$ 39,90

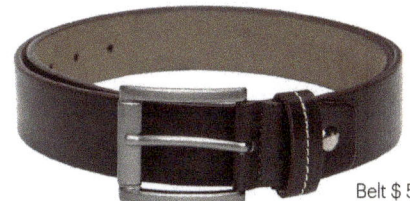

Trousers $ 99,90

Shoes $ 245

Ties (each)
$ 59,90

Belt $ 59,90

Pocket Squares (each) $ 39,90

THE POWER OF THE POCKET SQUARE

A pocket square goes a long way! In a jacket pocket, as a neck scarf, or tucked inside the pocket of a shirt or t-shirt, the pocket square comes in a variety of geometric prints and color combinations this season.

Ties (each) $ 59,90

NOTICE THE TIE

One of the great comebacks from the 80s is surely ties with girth. Make sure your knot is fairly loose and the length is longer than what you're used to – that's the only way to recreate the 80s look.

Coat $ 345,00

Belt $ 59,90

Trousers $ 99,90

Gloves $ 115,00

Blazer $ 295,00

Jacket $ 295,00

Sweatshirt
$ 89,90

Turtleneck Sweater
$ 89,90

TECHNO TOUCH

Performance fabrics no longer just belong to sportswear. While lightly padded puffer vests and bomber jackets have been a part of our collection for a couple of seasons now, we now see performance-wear fabrics in unexpected places such as a shirt collar or a jacket sleeve. One way to emphasize the surprise element of your key piece is to pair it with a more subdued wardrobe.

Folio $ 115,00

Shoes $ 245,00

Suit $ 495,00

Bow Tie $ 39,90

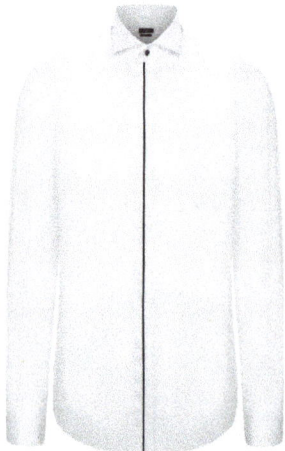

Shirt $ 99,90

Cufflink
$ 39,90

Trousers $ 89,90

Blazer $ 245,00

T-shirt $ 49,90

Trousers $ 89,90

CHOOSE YOUR LANE

A fashion season filled with stripes everywhere; but a single stripe really, on a t-shirt, a sweater, a jacket and even on accessories. Multi colored stripes strengthen any piece while maintaining a more casual look. Whether you combine all your striped pieces in one outfit, or pick and choose your lane is up to you.

Coat $ 245,00

Belt $ 49,90

Tie $ 59,90

Shoes $ 245,00

Vested suit $ 595,00

Coat $ 345,00

Shirt $ 89,90

Belt $ 49,90

Tie $ 59,90

Shoes $ 245,00

Coat
$ 495,00

Coat
$ 595,00

ASSERTIVE DETAILS

Faux fur is possibly the most important design detail that got added to overcoats this season. Those who like to stand out with their style will prefer this key wardrobe piece and can pair it with a more traditional three-piece suit in gray and other traditional colors.

Jacket $ 345,00

Belt $ 59,90

Trousers $ 99,90

Sweater $ 99,90

Trousers $ 99,90

Backpack $ 245,00

Socks
$ 9,90

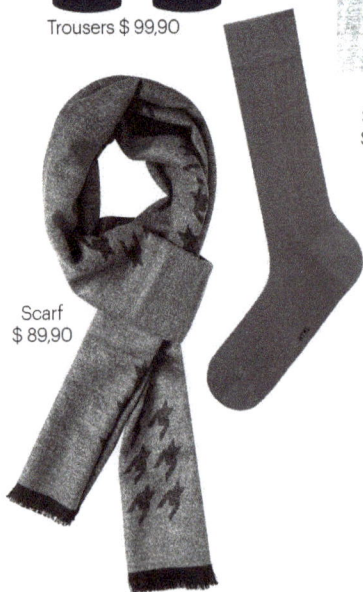

Scarf
$ 89,90

Boot $ 295,00

COLOR BLOCKS

We are very familiar with this fashion trend by now: color blocks are here to stay. This season, prepare to see large blocks of color creating more dramatic pieces. While contrast color blocking is still around, tone-on-tone options are also available.

SAYKI

SAYKI

THE RACE TO GENTLEMANLY STYLE

The key pieces of any dynamic and urban wardrobe arrive in stores with the 2017-18 Fall/Winter collections from Sayki. The Sayki gentleman updates his style this season without sacrificing from his impeccable style. Pinstripe fabrics, double-breasted jackets and elegant overcoats are in favor in this collection, where navy and burgundy take centerstage. Three-piece suits, fur collars, wool cashmere coats and denim-inspired shirts are some of the must-haves of this year.

PHOTOGRAPED BY BELL SOTO **STYLED BY** ISE WHITE

25

Coat $ 395,00, Sweater $ 69,90
Vested suit $ 595,00

THE CAMEL
OVERCOAT IS
ONE OF THE KEY
MUST-HAVE
PIECES THIS
SEASON. A
PERFECT
MATCH WITH
BURGUNDY.

Coat $ 495,00, Sweater $ 69,90,
Scarf $ 89,90, Trousers $ 125,00

Model on the left, Coat $ 495,00, Blazer $ 345,00,
Sweater $ 69,90, Trousers $ 99,90, Gloves $ 115,00

Model on the right, Coat $ 495,00, Shirt $ 89,90,
Tie $ 59,90, Vest $ 145,00, Trousers $ 125,00,
Belt $ 59,90, Gloves $ 115,00

Model on the left, Coat $ 495,00, Blazer $ 345,00, Shirt $ 59,90, Tie $ 59,90, Trousers $ 99,90, Shoes $ 295,00
Model on the right, Coat $ 345,00, Sweater $ 89,90, Shirt $ 89,90, Tie $ 59,90, Trousers $ 99,90, Shoes $ 295,00, Backpack $ 195,00

SAYKI

Puffer $ 345,00, Folio $ 115,00, Sweater $ 69,90, Trousers $ 99,90, Scarf $ 49,90

FALL IN THE CITY

The style code of this season is surely comfort. The soft texture of these jackets and the functionality of parkas and trenchcoats are bolstered in navy and burgundy, the popular colors of the year.

PHOTOGRAPHED BY DİNÇER DİNÇ ●● **STYLED BY** YEŞİM SUÜLKER

Shoes $ 245,00, Blazer $ 295,00, Ties (each) $ 59,90, Sweater $ 69,90, Trousers $ 99,90

Topcoat $ 245,00, Trousers $ 99,90, Gloves $ 99,90, Pocket Squares (each) $ 39,90, Ties (each) $ 59,90, Belt $ 49,90, Shirt $ 59,90

Shoes $ 245,00, Tie $ 59,90, Trousers $ 99,90, Puffer $ 295,00, Sweater $ 89,90

38

Coat $ 345,00, Shirt $ 89,90, Belt $ 59,90, Vested suit $ 395,00

SAYKI

Coat $ 345,00, Sweater $ 69,90, Trousers $ 89,90, Pocket Square $ 39,90,
Backpack $ 195,00, Scarf $ 89,90

42

THE HARMONY
OF CONTRASTS

The fashion motto for every Sayki man is impeccable style, as
he expertly brings together the different colors and textures of
jackets, vests and pants from the 2017-18 Fall/Winter collection
in three-piece suits.

PHOTOGRAPHY BY BELL SOTO **STYLED BY** JOE WHITE

Model on the left, Coat $ 345,00,
Sweater $ 89,90, Trousers $ 99,90,
Boot $ 345,00, Scarf $ 49,90
Model on the right, Blazer $ 295,00,
Sweater $ 89,90, Shirt $ 69,90,
Trousers $ 89,90, Shoes $ 245,00,
Tie $ 49,90, Pocket Square $ 19,90

44

Coat $ 295,00, Sweater $ 69,90, Shirt $ 69,90, Trousers $ 99,90, Folio $ 135,00

BRING TOGETHER ALL SHADES OF GRAY WHILE HIGHLIGHTING
THE JACQUARD WEAVE PATTERNS IN KNITS THIS SEASON.

PAIR YOUR
FAVORITE SUIT
WITH A VEST – BUT
MAKE SURE THE
TEXTURE OR COLOR
IS NOT THE SAME.

48

Coat $ 345,00, Shirt $ 59,90, Tie $ 49,90, Sweater $ 89,90, Trousers $ 89,90, Shoes $ 295,00

Vested suit $ 395,00, Shirt $ 89,90, Tie $ 49,90, Pocket Square $ 19,90, Belt $ 49,90

Blazer $ 345,00, Sweater $ 89,90,
Shirt $ 59,90, Trousers $ 89,90, Tie $ 49,90,
Pocket Square $ 39,90

SAYKI

A PERSONAL TOUCH

It's time to personalize your suit style with accessories. Even if the colors or textures do not match, tie, pocket square, scarf and cufflinks details from the Sayki collection come together beautifully in plaid or paisley designs.

PHOTOGRAPHED BY DINCER DINC ●● **STİL EDİTÖRÜ** YESIM SUULKER

Pocket Squares (each) $ 39,90, Cufflink $ 39,90

Coat $ 345,00, Shirt $ 89,90, Tie $ 49,90, Shoes $ 245,00,
Trousers $ 89,90, Scarf $ 89,90

58

Suit $ 345,00, Shirt $ 89,90, Coat $ 295,00, Gloves $ 99,90, Pocket Square $ 39,90

Blazer $ 345,00, Shirt $ 89,90, Pocket Square $ 39,90

SAYKI

62

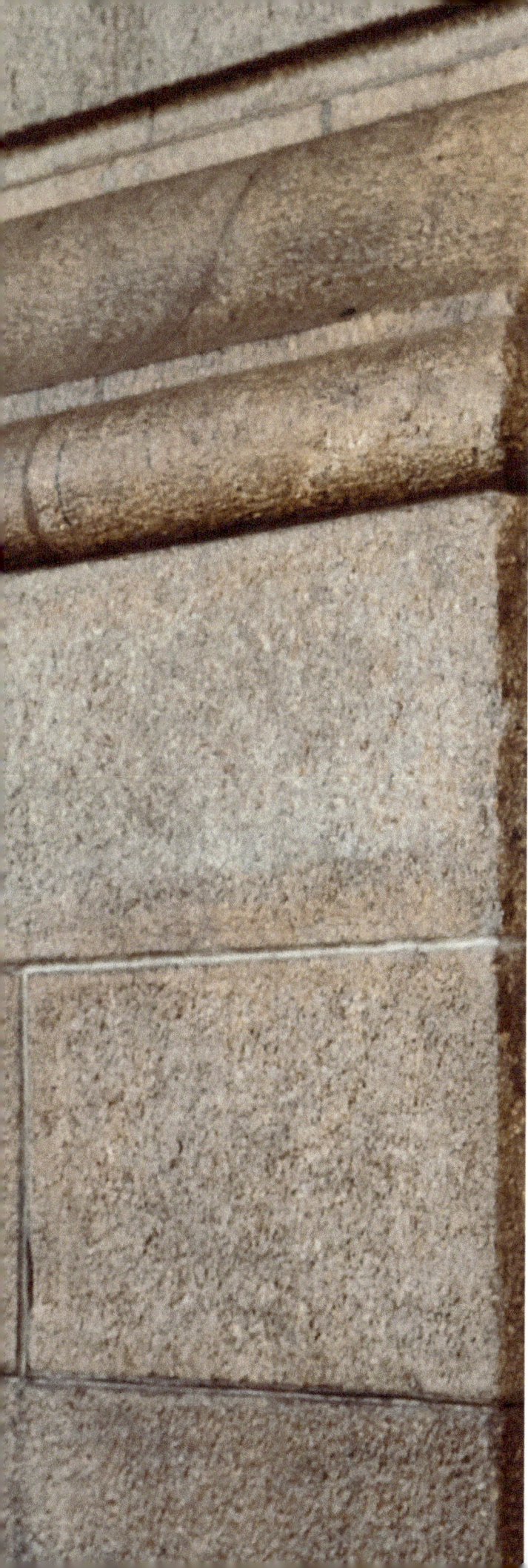

THE COMFORT ZONE

Play up your style this season with these determined, assertive pieces from Sayki. Find comfort in cargo pants, cowl neck knits, bomber jackets and quilted coats and that's your shortcut to the American dream.

PHOTOGRAPHY BELL SOTO
STYLED BY ISE WHITE

Vested suit $ 395,00, Shirt $ 89,90, Shoes $ 245,00, Belt $ 59,90

Coat $ 345,00, Suit $ 345,00,
Sweater $ 99,90, Backpack $ 245,00

WOOL CASHMERE CAMEL COATS
FEATURING WIDENING COLLARS MAY JUST BE
YOUR WARDROBE STAPLE.

Puffer $ 295,00, Vested suit $ 395,00, Shirt $ 89,90, Belt $ 59,90

Bomber Jacket $ 295,00, Sweater $ 89,90, Shirt $ 69,90,
Beanie $ 39,90, Jean $ 99,90, Shoes $ 295,00

HAIR BY MATTHEW TUOZZOLI **ART DIRECTOR** HALE GÜVENEN **MODELS** FILIP WOLFE, TREY GRILEY

Shirt $ 89,90, Backpack $ 245,00, Boot $ 345,00, Trousers $ 89,90

A MINIMALIST WINTER

It's all in the details when minimalist staples make up your Fall/Winter wardrobe. Sporty overcoats, quilted details and the perfectly coordinated navy, burgundy and gray pieces must make up the pieces you add to your collection this winter as you prepare for the changing weather.

PHOTOGRAPHED BY DINCER DINC ●● **STİL EDİTÖRÜ** YESIM SUULKER

70

Coat $ 395,00, Shirt $ 89,90, Trousers $ 99,90, Shoes $ 245,00

Shoes $ 245,00, Trousers $ 89,90, Coat $ 295,00, Shirt $ 89,90

Shoes $ 245,00, Shirt $ 89,90, Trousers $ 99,90, Gloves $ 115,00,
Coat $ 245,00, Belt $ 69,90

All black all the time with zipper details, leather pieces and texturized bomber jackets.

Trousers $ 99,90, Hoodie $ 89,90, Boot $ 295,00, Backpack $ 195,00

Coat $ 345,00, Trousers $ 99,90,
Socks (each) $ 19,90, Sweater $ 89,90

More black pieces are
part of the Sayki collections
this year than ever before.

Blazer $ 245,00, Trousers $ 99,90, Scarf $ 89,90, Folio $ 115,00

AN INVITATION TO COLOR

Patterns are back in eveningwear. Houndstooth tuxedos, suit jackets featuring velvet or satin collars and lapels, wool flannel fabrics in burgundy and charcoal all take centerstage at elegant gatherings. Play up your charismatic style with a new and updated look this year.

PHOTOGRAPHY BY BELL SOTO
STYLED BY ISE WHITE

Tuxedo $ 495,00, Shirt $ 99,90, Bow Tie $ 39,90

TRY A FITTED TURTLENECK SWEATER INSIDE YOUR
TUXEDO JACKET – NOW THAT'S STYLE.

Tuxedo $ 495,00, Bow Tie- Pocket Square Set $ 39,90, Shirt $ 89,90

Tuxedo $ 495,00, Shirt $ 115,00,
Bow Tie- Pocket Square Set $ 39,90,
Shoes $ 245,00

HAIR BY MATTHEW TUOZOLI ART DIRECTOR HALE GÜVENEN MODELS FILIP WOLFE, TREY GRILEY

Tie Clip $ 39,90, Cufflink $ 49,90, Shoes $ 245,00, Bow Tie $ 39,90, Shirt $ 115,00

AN ELEGANT STANCE

While an updated tuxedo from Sayki's 2017-18 Fall/Winter collection will prepare you for any occasion, make sure to personalize your style with key details like a bowtie, a cummerbund, cufflinks and a tie pin.

PHOTOGRAPHED BY DİNCER DINC ●● **STYLED BY** YESIM SUULKER

Tuxedo $ 495,00, Shirt $ 99,90, Bow Tie $ 39,90, Shoes $ 245,00

Tuxedo $ 595,00, Shirt $ 99,90, Bow Tie- Pocket Square Set $ 39,90, Belt $ 59,90, Shoes $ 245,00

Cummerbund- Bow Tie Set $ 69,90, Tie Clip $ 39,90, Shoes $ 245,00, Cufflink $ 39,90

Cummerbund- Bow Tie- Pocket Square Set $ 69,90, Belt $ 59,90, Shoes $ 245,00, Cufflink $ 59,90

87

SAYKI

Coat $ 245,00

Cruise often chooses to pair monochrome pieces together in a single look of casual pants, t-shirt and short zip-up, paired here with a pair of tone-on-tone brogues.

Boot $ 295,00

TOM CRUISE

Sweater $ 89,90

Trousers $ 99,90

91

MONOCHROME

He is the reigning star of cult action flicks and the honest citizen saving the world in doomsday movies. We can see the influence of all these characters on Tom Cruise's personal style. He follows trends without wavering from his classically casual fashion sense. While he doesn't take risks in clothes, we can see that he is consistent in maintaining a sporty chic look in his day-to-day.

Sweater $ 69,90

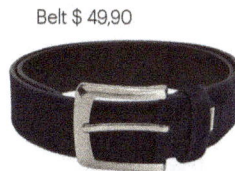

Belt $ 49,90

Backpack $ 195,00

Scarf $ 89,90

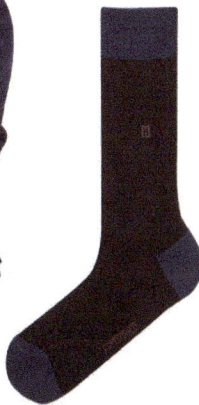

Socks $ 9,90

Gloves $ 115,00

Shirt $ 89,90

Cufflink $ 39,90

Belt $ 49,90

Blazer $ 295,00

*

A plaid gray two-piece suit make up Robert Downey Jr.'s look on this red carpet. He pairs his choice with one of the key pieces of the season: the wide vintage paisley tie.

ROBERT DOWNEY JR.

A STYLE OF PATTERNS

His Ironman character brought Robert Downey Jr.'s proven acting chops, up to cult status. While he maintains an extremely casual street style, Downey Jr. brings his A-game on special occasions. He's fearless in testing out seasonal fashion trends when creating his evening look and proves that he knows what he is doing. Playing with and combining prints in an elegant look is definitely his super power.

Tie $ 59,90

Shoes $ 245,00

Suit $ 495,00

Coat $ 245,00

Suit $ 495,00

HUGH JACKMAN

Vested Suit $ 595,00

A CLASSIC CHARISMA

Hugh Jackman always looks razor sharp. He chooses timeless pieces for both his everyday look as well as eveningwear choices. Unlike some of the characters he portrays, he cleans up as an impeccable gentleman when in one of his fitted suits.

Tie $ 59,90

Socks $ 9,90

Shoes $ 245,00

Australian actor Hugh Jackman pairs his pinstripe suit with a crisp white dress shirt and a classic tie on this occasion. His flawless haircut, paired with a confident stance and attitude, is the perfect companion to his gentlemanly look.

Shirt $ 89,90

Belt $ 59,90

ISTANBUL IN TWO DAYS

The city shows a different face to each visitor and even in two days, you can discover so much as you explore through the streets. Each day has its own itinerary below so come follow in our footsteps.

BY ÇİĞDEM TOPARLAK

THE BOSPHORUS

We start with breakfast at Emek Café in Yenikoy, a local favorite right on the water. "Menemen" is definitely the house specialty, delicious runny scrambled eggs cooked with fresh tomatoes, green peppers and butter. Make sure to order a potato stuffed "borek" on the side; it looks like an empanada but trust us—the recipe is kept in utmost secrecy and cannot be replicated. If you're looking for a more upscale destination, why not try Molka, also in Yenikoy, with a slightly more sophisticated menu. Another local favorite, the chef here masterfully combines regional specialties like "bazlama," or Turkish flatbreads, with international choices like eggs benedict.

As you make your way down the Bosphorus, take a break in Emirgan at the Sakip Sabanci Museum and check out the Ai WeiWei exhibition. The museum building is one of the oldest settlements on the Bosphorus, also known as "Atlı Köşk," (The Mansion with the Horse) and provides visitors with amazing views of the city through its tiered gardens and outdoor spaces. The restaurant can also provide pleasant surprises as it's a partnership project with The Culinary Arts Academy (MSA) in Istanbul. Then again right next door is Emirgan's famous Sutis where you may want to try the "tavuk gogsu," the creamy chicken breast pudding. Another must-stop-and-drink-tea locale is Emirgan Cinaralti, which often appears in lyrics of local melodies.

If you're not a risk taker when it comes to dessert, maybe you'll want to take a ferry across the Bosphorus to Kanlica to try the local yogurt and honey concoction. Those whose curiosity is peaked by the Anatolian side should continue down the coast and visit Kuzguncuk, one of the oldest and most beautiful Istanbul neighborhoods. If you choose to go back to the European side, head on to Rumeli Hisari where a magnificent fortress awaits you. The hillside that graces

SPICE MARKET

the portion of the Bosphorus where the water is the most tumultuous is Asiyan. There you'll not only find the Rumeli Hisari fortress walls but also the Tevfik Fikret Museum. Down the coast is Bebek, a posh neighborhood where it's possible to run into a Turkish celebrity at every corner. Continuing our food journey, try the "Bebek Badem Ezmesi," (almond paste) sold in local stores and head on over to Bebek Café to enjoy it with your Turkish coffee. Another alternative is to enjoy the view while sitting on a bench under the some of the oldest trees in Bebek Park. If you're familiar with Turkish movies from the 60s, the bar at Bebek Hotel will also delight.

After quick stops in Arnavutkoy and Kurucesme, it's time to venture into Ortakoy. Stuffed baked potatoes enjoyed in the shadow of the Nigogos Balyan's Mosque of Grand Mecidiye (Buyuk Mecidiye Camii) is must for any Istanbul explorer. Then you must walk, hopefully burning some of the calories consumed with the baked potato, from Ortakoy to Besiktas and track the footsteps of the Ottoman officials at the end of 19th century. If you want to experience the true essence of palaces along the Bosphorus, why not catch tea time at the Gazebo Lounge in the Ciragan Palace Kempinski Hotel and greet the memory of Ataturk, the founder of modern Turkey, at the Dolmabahce Palace. And if you're into soccer, a commemorative

GAZEBO LOUNGE

BASILICA SISTERN

HAMDI RESTAURANT

MODA

visit to the Besiktas store in Vodafone arena is a must do. Before the end of the day, you might just have enough time to stop by the sole contemporary art museum of the city, Istanbul Modern, and view the 15th Istanbul Biennial this fall. That's enough walking; park yourself at Ferah Feza to bid goodnight to all as you enjoy one of the most breathtaking rooftop views of the city. The menu of this unique culinary experience is brand new this fall and the terrace offers the perfect place to watch the spectacular sunset. If you still have room at the end of the day, dessert should definitely be "baklava" from neighboring Karakoy Gulluoglu.

THE OLD TOWN

While most Old Town walking tours start at the Hagia Sophia (Ayasofya Camii) we'll take off from the Tower of Galata and the walls of Genovese. First we stop for breakfast either at the Setup Café in Kabatas or the Firuzaga Tea House in Cihangir, the latter frequented by actors who live in the neighborhood. Afterwards, you can walk through backstreets also seen in old Kemal Sunal movies, especially Gunesli Sokak (name of the street), and reach the Tower of Galata by way of Istiklal Caddesi (the main strip heading down from Taksim Square.) Down towards the water via the Komando Staircase and Bankalar Caddesi, the street also known for housing the Salt Galata, the Museum of the Bank of the Ottomans (Osmanli Bankasi Muzesi,) and Anna Laudel Contemporary destinations. Then you'll stroll over the Galata Bridge and into the historical peninsula. You can feed the birds in front of the New Mosque (Yeni Camii), sample

spices at the Egyptian Spice Market (Misir Carsisi) and purchase the best Turkish coffee from Kuru Kahveci Mehmet Efendi. Balat is a must-see detour if you want to see the awe-inspiring tiles from the Byzantine period at the Kariye Museum. You can also stop by Eyup Sultan and Pierre Loti while in this neighborhood.
Venturing deep into Old Town, you'll find the famous Vefa Bozacisi in the neighborhood of Vefa. Boza is a fermented Turkish drink made of bulgur and yeast, with a slightly sweet and tangy flavor. Roasted chickpeas are the perfect accompaniment as you head over to the Suleymaniye Mosque and Kulliye, designed by the famous Turkish architect Mimar Sinan. Restaurant Nar is a slightly more upscale dining option in Nurosmaniye as you follow the tram tracks to the Corlulu Ali Pasha Medrese for a cup of Turkish coffee.
Sultanahmet Square is the shining glory of history at the end of your tour of the Old Town. Everywhere you turn, you'll find a piece of history you'll want to explore from the Basilica Cistern, the Sultanahmet Mosque, Hagia Sophia Museum and the Topkapi Palace. Fountains, obelisks and other rock monuments found in the Square will also take your breath away. The Little Hagia Sophia Mosque, originally built by Byzantine Emperor Justinian the First, is also right here. After your time in Sultanahmet Square, you can follow the tram tracks head down to the Sirkeci train station. You'll find the Istanbul Archeology Museum, the Islamic Science Center and Gulhane Park on the way. When you're at sea level once again, you must end the day at Hamdi restaurant with a delicious meal of Turkish pistachio kebap.

About Moda

One of the hottest neighborhoods in Istanbul at the moment is located on the Anatolian side. The young intellectuals all hang out in Moda these days, traveling from all over Istanbul and returning home at the end of the day. Arriving via a short ferry ride from the European side to Kadikoy and walking about 15 minutes to arrive in Moda is all you need to do to enjoy the neighborhood's modern cafes, theatres and good-looking crowd. Sunset at the Moda Tea House is very special. If you're starting your day, you can also enjoy brunch at Moda Brunelle and ice cream at Yasar Usta's place. 180 Degree coffee offers delicious coffee drinks as you make your way through the unique boutiques like Wunder Moda and Zelazo along your route. And why not pay a visit to the Baris Manco Home Museum, dedicated to the famous Turkish rock musician who passed away in 1999.

New York New York

It's true that this city never sleeps. To tour New York like a local take this guide along with you as you explore Chelsea with its art galleries, Flatiron with its inventive culinary experiences and East Village with its art and culture.

BY AHU TERZI

They call it the city that never sleeps. It's not hard to imagine why. The lights at Times Square are on all night, the pizza places open for 24 hours and the nightlife in the West Village often lasts until the sun rises. Most of Manhattan is up all day and night. When Fall arrives, the city comes alive even more. Once school starts, the arts and culture in the city also comes to life with new programming at museums and theatres. It gets harder and harder to find a seat on Broadway or a spot to squeeze into at live music events. Yet, it's still possible to experience a quieter New York by leaving the touristic spots behind and enjoying neighborhoods favored by the locals. You won't even have to leave the neighborhood where you're staying. With this guide, you'll still enjoy New York to the fullest.

CHELSEA

Designed into the train tracks originally built above Manhattan in 1934, the High Line Park helped this neighborhood complete its transition into a desirable destination. With its hip art galleries on 26th street, concept stores that house pop-up shops and innovative restaurants, Chelsea is must-visit during your New York visit. The wanderers dream destination Chelsea Market is within walking distance. The neighborhood also boasts an Apple Store and provides easy access to the vibrant nightlife in the Meatpacking District. One of the most interesting hotels you can choose for your trip is The High Line Hotel. (thehighlinehotel.com) This brick building originally erected atop local poet Clement Clarke's apple orchard, the hotel charms not only with its history but also luxurious details. If you can spare the time, grab one of the Shinola bicycles reserved for hotel guests and ride up the Hudson River Park bike path, located a short distance from the hotel. Leaves will be changing colors as you take in the stunning views of the Hudson River. Other destinations to add to your list are Sullivan Street Bakery, 192 Books, Gagosian Gallery and Foragers Market, all within a short walking distance to the hotel. If you happen to be staying there on October 31st, make sure to check out the Halloween costume party for dogs. Another date to add to the calendar is November 29th when the hotel hosts a tree lighting ceremony in its mesmerizing garden to celebrate the holiday season with its guests. Hot chocolate, spiced cider and carolers will greet you as you head back to your room from a day out in the neighborhood.

Of course you can't not visit the High Line Park if you're staying at the High Line Hotel. Lining up the western coast of the island of Manhattan, the Park starts at 34th street in the North and ends at the Whitney Museum in the South. Plants and flowers brought in from all over the Hudson Valley are clearly identified along your path as you make your way downtown, accompanied by art installations and sculptures by artists from around the world. And of course, the Whitney Museum will be waiting for you at the end of your walk. One of the most anticipated exhibitions of the 2017 Fall season is Brazilian artist Hélio Oiticica's show.

FLATIRON

If Chelsea is known with its art galleries, then Flatiron is definitely the destination for some of the most inventive culinary experiences available in New York. We'll start with The Library, voted the best hotel bar in New York, located at the NoMad Hotel and exclusively reserved for hotel guests after 4 pm every day. In fact, the NoMad should be your hotel of choice if you choose to stay in the Flatiron neighborhood. Famous French designer Jacques Garcia decorated all 168 rooms of this hotel with claw-footed tubs, rich fabrics and hand knotted vintage rugs. The hotels famous drinks were created by Leo Robitschek, also known as the genius behind Eleven Madison Park, and can be enjoyed not only in the library but also at the rooftop terrace or in front of a cozy fireplace in the lobby. (thenomadhotel.com)

Here, every meal can be a date with a famous

CHRISTINA QUARLES /ICP

HALLOWEEN COSTUME
PARTY FOR DOGS

THE BOWERY HOTEL / EAST VILLAGE

chef. French Le Coq Rico (lecoqriconyc.com), modern Mexican Cosme (cosmenyc.com) and Michelin-starred British chef Jason Atherton's Clocktower (theclocktowernyc.com) are some of our favorite destination restaurants. When in New York, you must also try sushi. Legendary sushi chef Kazunori Nozawa detests American style sushi rolls and serves up only the freshest as part of his "Trust Me" menu at his first New York City outpost of L.A.-based Sugarfish. The restaurant doesn't take reservations so unless you're OK with waiting 2-3 hours for dinner, make sure to arrive by 5 when you'll be seated after a short wait. Order one of the Trust Me menus and ask the waiter to slow down the service. Chef Nozawa's sushi delights can only be enjoyed when you truly devour every bite.

EAST VILLAGE

While you may run into a tourist or two in Chelsea or the Flatiron, East Village is truly the locals' neighborhood. Our hotel choice in this neighborhood is The Bowery. (theboweryhotel.com) Don't spend too much time in your room, however, as you'll have a lot to see at the New museum and the International Center of Photography (ICP) nearby. Among the 40 artists represented at the New Museum's upcoming mixed exhibition this Fall is Christina Quarles. The exhibition explores the effect of gender and sexuality on popular culture

and is already receiving a lot of exciting press. Another important installation is Kahlil Joseph's short films also at the New Museum. (newmuseum.com) The International Center of Photography is across the street from the New Museum, on the west side of the Bowery. A must see at the ICP this Fall is Lauren Greenfield's Generation Wealth. More than 200 photographs from the artists collection will be shown as part of the exhibition, representing over 25 years of Greenfield's work among the rich and famous. With subjects ranging from American to locals in Ireland, Iceland, Saudi Arabia, China and Russia, the photographers work spans cultures, attitudes as well as professions. The show specifically highlights how the American Dream has changed in the 21st century and whether it's still achievable in the traditional sense. (www.icp.org) Both the New Museum and the ICP are closed on Mondays but open until late on Thursdays. After you enjoy your art-filled day, why not try dinner at Le Coucou, which one the Best Restaurant award in the James Beard competition this year. American Chef Daniel Rose got his fame in Paris but now brings his culinary expertise to the Lower East side. Our favorite items on the menu are the lamb chops and the leeks. (lecoucou.com) You can spend another one of your nights at Joe's Pub, a live music venue that is part of the Public Theater. (publictheater.org)

When in New York...

Why not stop by at one of Sayki's stores to experience elevated midtown style with timeless pieces from our 2017-18 Fall/Winter collection. At both the Madison Avenue location near popular tourist destination Grand Central Station, and the Woodbury Common Premium Outlets, a short drive from Manhattan, you'll find an excellent selection of suits in most up-to-date styles. Our customer service is unparalleled allowing you to truly enjoy designing your own style whether you are shopping for a few key pieces or an entire wardrobe.

MIDTOWN
340 Madison Ave. (Between 43rd and 44th Street) New York, NY 10017
+1 212 661 7600 Monday-Saturday: 9 AM – 7 PM Sunday: 12 PM – 6 PM

WOODBURY COMMON
PREMIUM OUTLETS
264 Red Apple Ct. suite #264 Central Valley, NY 10917
+1 845 928 1065
Monday-Saturday: 9 AM – 7 PM
Sunday: 12 PM – 6 PM

FOLLOW TO WIN

FOLLOW US ON INSTAGRAM AND FACEBOOK, LEAVE YOUR COMMENTS ON GOOGLE+ AND YELP FOR A CHANCE TO WIN SURPRISE GIVEAWAYS.

yelp G+ ⬡ f /sayki1924

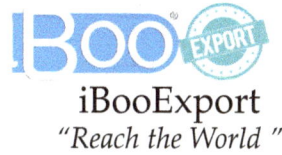

iBooExport
"Reach the World "

Istanbul Office	London Office
EGS Business Park	3rd Floor
B2 Blok No: 12 D.01	86-90 Paul Street
Yesilkoy, Bakirkoy,	London
İstanbul 34149	EC2A 4NE
Turkey	United Kingdom
t: +90 850 460 1 064	t: +44 20 3828 7097

info@ibooexport.com II www.ibooexport.com

ISBN

978-1-947144-68-2 (sc)
978-1-947144-69-9 (e)

We care about the environment. This paper used in this publication is both acid-free and totally chlorine-free (TCF). It meets the minimum requirements of ANSI/NISO z39.48-1992 (r 1997)

Printed in the USA